Coming Home

Tara Davis

COMING HOME

ISBN: 978-1-946106-34-6

DEDICATION

Mom and Dad, thank you for giving
me the greatest gift ever: Jesus.

TARA DAVIS

FOREWORD

It is with great pleasure I recommend this devotional to you. The author, Tara Davis, is not only an example of a woman not unlike King David, who tirelessly seeks after God's heart, but of whom is also a servant being grateful for her portion of grace which compels her to serve. She is a beautiful and strong woman of God.

Though raised in a Christian home, her life has been broken through family conflict, her own poor choices including drugs, alcohol, and the belief that God did not and could not love her. As Tara wrestles daily with her own personal challenges, she has continually found that God has renewed her strength in her reflection on him and the Grace he has shown, now she shares some of her stories of COMING HOME to strengthen others who seek a stronger relationship with God. Her ministry is to us all as we face our own challenges.

Enjoy the peace Tara reminds her readers of, God's got this!

Karen Estep, Ph.D.
Doctoral Chair
Grand Canyon University

TARA DAVIS

CONTENTS

TARA DAVIS

ACKNOWLEDGMENTS

Aunt Wilma, you were the constant voice cheering me on to take that first courageous step. I'm forever grateful.

The one who knows me far better than all others, my better half and twin sister Sara - Thank you for believing in me from the beginning. You've never swayed from helping others live out their dreams.

Edie, my publisher, the countless ways in which you promote Jesus and His Kingdom are inspiring beyond words. Thank you! This wouldn't exist without you.

To all of my friends who have faithfully prayed me through, cheered me on, and been so gracious to read anything I've ever written. I truly lack words. Your faith fans the flame within me, thank you! We are better together!

Thank you to my friends, family, and coworkers at House of Faith. What a joy it is to serve alongside each of you. The best is yet to come!

Special thanks to my professor, friend and mentor, Dr. Karen Estep for writing the Foreword to this book. I look up to you far more than you realize! Thank you for allowing Jesus to rescue me through the selfless ways you served and loved me at my worst.

Thank you to Joy for the front cover photograph; and to my family at The Christian Church of San Angelo for always standing behind me in your words, love, prayers, and actions. Isabelle, thank you so much for helping with finishing touches and edits under the pressure of a deadline.

When you find friends that will quote your own sermons back to you, you've found a gift. Bird and Brooks, here's to countless convertible rides, retreats with rice, and running this race together. I'm better because the Lord has so graciously allowed our paths to cross in the most fun and surprising of ways! Thank you for being friends that are like family in the best of ways.

Sierra, Eva, Pratater, and Barker clan, I love you more than words can say.

I'd like to thank my hero, Jesus Christ. Every ounce of praise, honor and glory belongs to Him. He is the reason for any good that you see in me. He has been so faithful when I have not. I am my Beloved's and He is mine, such a gift and honor to just be His.

1 A NATIVITY OF NECESSITY

I'll be honest. I have been peeking in through the dusty window all weekend. I hear the cries of the animals. I see the reverence of the wise men. I smell the country air, and feel the chill on my arm as my heart is captured. My eyes are captivated with just one glance. I feel at home here. I sense a deep peace within this place, a place I have never known.

Wait a minute! I have to go. I need to run. I don't belong here! The darkness surrounds me, and the violent threats of death echo deep within my weary soul. I have nothing to give this King, born in the most humble of places. My life is like mere shattered glass. It is rough on the edges and full of pain. This King is worthy of so much more.

Then, I feel the light begin to break through, shining into my unending darkness. Am I fit for the courts of a King? No. Does a King belong in a stable? No. Nonetheless, here He is, and here am I. In this moment, heaven and earth collide. This is the wonderful mystery of this place I'm learning to call *home*.

Full of waste? Yes. Surrounded by darkness? Yes. In places I'd never choose to go? Yes. What is the difference here? My God is here. My King Jesus has come into my world. Amidst the chaos, and in spite of unfavorable circumstances, here He is.

He is here! My long awaited, promised One. His very presence beckons me closer still. With aching feet and tear-stained cheeks, I come inside. The more I gaze at His sweet face, the more everything around me begins to fade.

Yes, I am home. My Beloved and I. Thank you for coming, Christ child. I have been waiting. Welcome to my chaos. It is You who brings me peace.

2 THE GREAT ROAR

Broken shards of life, shattered by pain. "Mosaic of mercy and beauty, I give you a new name."

Tears unending and heart full of wrath. "Look, my beloved! I've been carving for you a new path." Fists clenched, and eyes distracted with lust. "Come to Me now, My child! Come quickly. You must!"

Darkness closes in. The doubt begins to soar. Body trembling, my breath taken away, I finally hear His great roar! "Where are we going, Aslan? Please stop! Wait for me!" Tired feet quicken, and weary heart now beating more quickly.

The further we run the brighter it gets. I feel a stirring of courage deep within my chest. Jumping on His back, with my weary hands clinging to His mane so long, He roars with power so swift! I begin to hear a new song. "Come away with Me, my beloved, to a land full of light. It's time to leave the cover of dark, and the familiar mask of night."

I see trees where once there was unending char. He won't slow down. We must be going far! New blossoms upon branches with leaves so green. This is the most beautiful of places I have ever seen. The stars glisten with a hope I've never known. "Ah yes, my Aslan! You are taking me home."

Listen and be still, and you too will hear His voice. You must wait, and stand, and listen through the noise. Yes! He is coming to carry you away. Just one moment with Him, and you'll never be the same.

He roars and I laugh, as the wind blows our every hair. Oh, what a rich inheritance I have, a most generous share. Riding upon the back of the One who conquers my every last fear, this is it! His majestic roar is what I have been waiting to hear.

The darkness collides with light and day is birthed from night. A most heavenly of collisions is now taking place. It is He who bears the divine incision, and roars with powerful grace.

3 WINTER CABIN

The journey's been long. Winter beats upon my back. It's funny how you can carry more baggage home than that with which you left. The snow is thick and the wind whips relentlessly. The excitement grows within my heart. I'm almost home!

I climb up rickety cabin steps, frozen over with the bitter ice of winter, and kick my hardened heels to shake off the remnants of a journey far too long. Walking in, I give my usual greeting, only to hear my voice echo in the empty hollows. The fireplace - not a trace of embers, no smoke billowing. It's as cold as death in here.

Where are my friends? My family? My Father? Have I no home here in this place? My heart sinks. Where is the fire that once burned hot? Where is the Father welcoming me home? I had just set down these heavy bags. My hands are calloused with carrying a burden I was never meant to carry.

I begin to lace up my boots again. I start to bundle back up for another long, lonely journey of wandering. Then I hear it! The crackle of a fire. I step into the Great Room and there They sit: the Father, Son and Spirit. And the fire! Oh, it's beautiful, and so majestic! It's so much greater now, much bigger. The heat encompasses the whole cabin.

I laugh with delight and run into my Father's arms. I am home. I am safe. But where are the others? The ones who once filled this cabin? Have they too quit, like so many others who have gone before?

Then You grab my hand to lead me to the window. Using Your hands that created the world, You wipe the frost from the window pane. Then I see it - a village! An entire village with so many cabins, all with smoke billowing from fires that burn. What was once a cabin is now a village.

My heart is stirred! I'm home again, and You, oh God, are growing, and multiplying, these remnants. The fires are greater, the cabins more. We are not alone. The fire has not gone out.

4 A BROKEN HEART HOME

You have made Yourself a home out of this broken heart. Opening the door to let You in was my only part. The floors, they creak, and the faucets, they leak, but You have come - gentle of heart, and lovely, and meek. Holes litter the walls like reminders of promises broken, hope and redemption and freedom -- this is what You have now spoken.

You come, You deliver, You restore. Herein, with You, I've found my forever home. It's different now, much different than it once was. You'd think I'd hosted the most royal of guests. Ah, yes, how quickly I seem to relapse! My sin, which once so easily entangled, has now been buried with my past.

New paint, new floors, even cupboards stocked to the brim. When they ask what happened, I say it was all Him! The way your house can be so broken with windows barred shut, it was You and You alone, You were all I had left. But You came and You delivered and

You restored me to what I was meant to be. Me here with You, and You here with me, in the end of it all........I am finally free.

5 THE CROSS THAT BLEEDS

Recent weeks have proven to be a challenge in many ways. One particular night I was wrestling, shifting around and trying to rearrange a matter in such a way that it would bring relief. Then it hit me; this is what Christ Himself has called us to: deny ourselves, and pick up our cross daily.

I wonder what it would have been like if the cross that Christ laid His life upon would have been comfortable. Would any blood have been spilt? Would any sacrifice have truly been made? Would it feed into the mockery, and the lies, of an enemy who has continuously perpetuated the Kingdom of God into a big joke? Would He have risen to conquer death, once and for all?

So it is with us, this idea of a cross that is to be picked up daily. It can no longer be paraded around like a pretty charm, and a beautiful centerpiece. It is death - a continual dying to ourselves. There will be blood, sweat, and tears; there will be pain and anguish. But there cannot be comfort, for we await the One who is greater, the Holy Spirit. He is the One who will bring comfort - He is comfort.

Those who lay their lives upon the cross will rise again, but with faces that mirror the holiness of Christ, and hearts that radiate with His righteousness. Wrestling to get comfortable? Settle. Only be still and know that He is God. In due season, you will rise: brand new, justified, and righteous in Christ. You will have overcome!

Those who lose their lives find their life. This is the way of the cross that bleeds.

6 SET APART

I've been parked in Leviticus for a while. It is striking to me the number of times God reminds the Israelites, "I am Yahweh, who sets you apart as holy." It seems like anytime I try to set a living creature just right for a picture, be it my dog or a baby, a mishap occurs. The dog runs off or the baby crawls away.

So it is with us. God has called us, even commanded us, to be holy. He sets us apart to be holy, and time after time we miss the mark. We run after broken cisterns that never satisfy; we chase after our own pleasures, and determine who it is we will be. I am struck at the patience of the Father ... the mercy and grace with which He deals so lovingly with each one of us. Picking us up again, He sets us apart.

Any photographer will tell you that it's the darkness that produces the light in pictures. God, in His incredible Self, is the only One who can take any negative and turn it into a positive.

Maybe it's not so much that God sets us apart to be holy because He is stiff-necked and cold hearted, but maybe it's much different. Actually, it is different. God sets us apart, because He wants to produce in us, pixel by pixel, a pure picture of Who He is, so that all the world may know that He is God, and He is good. To remind the world waiting in darkness that evil never wins.

7 PRODIGAL ME

Your love never ending … Your grace never failing … Redemption is calling us home.

There He stood, Father calling the prodigals home. The wayward drunk, the desperate addict, the worthless prostitute. Upon returning, the other son comes with an attitude as stiff as his heart! "But why Father? You're giving him the robe? A ring? A feast? A party? This same one who squandered his inheritance? What about me, I haven't squandered a thing?"

Oh, yes, My child. You have. You have squandered my greatest sacrifice by thinking you can earn my favor and love. You've squandered my worship by creating an idol of yourself, your good works, and your accomplishments. Redemption is calling you home. You've been bought with a price, and for a price; you are destined for greater than this.

Perhaps the prodigal wasn't a story about the wayward

others; but, instead, it was a story about selfish, prideful me. Your love never ending … Your grace never failing… Redemption is calling us home.

Redemption is calling me home.

8 WANDERING DOG AND RUNAWAY HEARTS

Sometimes your heart can be so far from truth that you don't even know where it is. Little lies can slip in through the cracks, and make themselves at home. Before you know it, there are giants in your land and you've made yourself a home in the land of unbelief.

A huge thunder clap awoke me this morning, and that is when I saw it…the front door cracked open. My dog was missing! The rain was intense, and the wipers were on high speed as I called a friend to help. My tears were now in sync with the rain that beat relentlessly against my windshield. They kept saying, "You're going to find him."

The entire time, I kept thinking to myself, "You don't know my dog the way I know him; he runs like a horse, is as stubborn as me, and 'come' is a concept that has never registered in his brain. You just don't know my dog, not to mention he doesn't have his collar and tags on."

My heart sank as I braced myself to find his dead body on the street, until I came around a corner and saw a police car turning slowly down my alley with my pup following. There were tears, there was laughter! After a much needed conversation about the dangers of leaving home, about which I'm sure he could care less, there was a sleeping dog on my bed. Most importantly, my heart had been awakened to this, "If God can find lost dogs, God can find lost souls."

We all know people who are lost - desperately lost - sometimes so far from the truth that they don't even know it. After a season of great loss on every level, I had forgotten who God truly was. Is He not big enough to rescue the least of these? To deliver the most bound among us? To find the ones whom others have forgotten about and dismissed? After all, God sees and knows all, and as a matter of fact, there is nothing too hard for Him.

The sun began to crack through dark storm clouds that once lingered overhead. There is a breaking forth of light among the darkness, as if God Himself is saying, "I'm not done here yet."

Don't stop believing. Trust that God loves, and knows more intimately, your friends and family than you do; and never stop praying. It's funny how a wandering dog can bring a runaway heart back home.

9 AN OCEAN OF GRACE

I've been thinking a lot this weekend, about a lot of things. I have so much junk, a desperately wicked heart, and incredible feelings of loneliness. Today was one of those days I'd rather not repeat, for lots of reasons; primarily, because sin hurts, and so often, we wound one another in the middle of our mess.

I've been floating in this huge ocean and have been thinking about Peter: how he walked on the water, and of course Jesus calmed the storms. There are so many other Bible stories I've heard over the years. Whether it was a good story or a bad story, there's one thing that remained true - Christ was always there.

I'm a runner. I have dreamed more and more about taking flight and recreating my life elsewhere, because it would just be easier. It would be much easier to quit and self-sabotage with sin. Sometimes holding out for hope and joy seems impossible, almost unnatural in a sense - much like climbing out of a boat in the middle of the sea. But in the end, it comes down to this: I want to be where Jesus is, because that is the only place I have ever found joy, love and peace. In Christ is the only place I've ever found a place to belong.

So know this - God is with you and for you and loves you! He hasn't given up and He is still big enough to save the day! There is nothing to fear because He is always with you. You can be brave because He isn't finished yet. You can be weak because He is strong. You can cry because He catches your every tear in a bottle. You can be broken because He makes beauty out of broken. You can question because He always answers. You can rest because He never does. You simply cannot quit because He won't let you! We are in this together, and better together.

It is ironic how alone I've felt in the middle of this ocean, saltwater drying out my skin as my unbelief dries out my own little heart. I've been questioning and asking God, "Where are You?" And then I hear the faintest of whispers, "I AM here. I hold the oceans of the world in my hands."

I am left undone, in the middle of this ocean, in the hands of my Maker.

10 LOVE ALWAYS WINS

I'm on vacation this week, visiting dear friends, and surrounded by pastures. This morning I find myself sitting in a doctor's office, waiting, and thinking about the friend I'm about to go visit who was just diagnosed with leukemia. I've been chatting with a business woman who works in the social enterprise realm, has a team she collaborates with all over the world, and is a national speaker, as well as named the number two leader of the year. Big words are flying everywhere and I'm trying to stay engaged and follow along, but she's losing me.

She then asks me, "What do you use?" Translation within context – "What do you do to share life and knowledge with people?" I'm struck, wishing I could crawl under this chair, altogether too small to contain the entirety of me.

Sheepishly, I say, "You know, the basics - Instagram, Twitter, Snapchat, Facebook." But it has me thinking…how exactly do I do this thing called life? I constantly feel behind the curve on social media, and way too advanced when it comes to productivity. Somewhere along the way I've lost the ability to simply play, to laugh, to dance freely under the stars. When did connecting with people become about platforms, and performance, instead of pleasure and relationship?

I'm being reminded this week about the simplicity of it all, how it's best to simply love others and in turn to receive their love. How in the middle of highways and byways of the busyness of life, there is a Shepherd who still leads us besides streams of water, and makes us to lie down in green pastures. How it never matters just how many followers I have, but rather the One I follow. The amount of likes can never compare to the love I receive from my Father. There can be questions without answers, and silence is only awkward when you don't say what you need to say.

There are moments too dark for even the quickest of snaps, and memories you'd never want to Instagram, but there are people whom God has graced us with that I'd never want anywhere else than by my side. For that I am thankful.

It's when we use love, the greatest gift of all, that we are made better, stronger, more beautiful. I am hopeful, challenged, and inspired, that the next time I am posed that question I can answer quietly, courageously, and unashamedly, "I use love."

After all, to be known is to be loved, and to be loved is to be known. Who doesn't crave to know that they are loved just as they are? Yes, He restores my soul. 'Tis so sweet to trust in my Jesus.

11 ADRIFT

This year has been a season of not experiencing the presence of God like I typically do, something that's been at times difficult to navigate in my walk with the Lord. A few weeks ago I was floating in the middle of an ocean, having this conversation with God. The poem below was birthed out of this experience.

The waves they toss to and fro
Crashing in like the tempest of winds
The skies grow dark and clouds linger near
Doubt creeps in and dances with fear
I begin to wonder where it is You've gone
When will my weary heart sing a new song
It seems as though I've been out here all alone
No place to dream, no place to call home

Trying to keep myself above the waves I wonder if
Your mighty hand, does it still save
In a moment of desperation I finally cry out,
"Where are You God?"

The silence that comes quickly after leaves my heart like
dry, cracked sod
But then Your still small voice with such
tenderness whispers
My child, come close while My presence still lingers
I AM that I AM and the oceans of this world I hold in
My hand
You may feel alone in the middle of this vast sea
But what you've forgotten is who holds it all together,
it is Me
When again you forget and wonder where I AM
Just remember you are My child,
you rest in My hands

12 When a Groom Asks

I've been all over the place the last two months, experiencing many different levels of life. This past Friday, I found myself lakeside, at the wedding of someone I didn't even know. A friend had invited me to go with her and her family to a relative's wedding. I was at the reception, tired and fighting many battles that raged within. There I sat with makeup on my face, enough hairspray and pins in my hair to wage a war, and wearing a skirt of all things in the middle of lots of people...people I didn't even know. I was uncomfortable to the tenth degree.

In a quick glance after dinner the groom looked at me and asked, "Are you having fun?" A smile broke out, and it was one of those moments where you answer by faith, rather than fact. As he walked away, it struck me - the groom just asked me if I was having fun at his party! And it's stayed with me now for several days. This was a delightful bit of fresh manna to chew on.

I've been reflecting on Jesus, when He said He, "prepares a table" for me. A table is an invitation to come and feast, and a table prepared by Christ is an invitation to fellowship. Sure, the enemies lurk and the lies never stop chasing us down. Wars rage and unrest fills our streets more than the masses do, but it's in the midst of that where a table is prepared.

The news headlines are nothing more than a daily reminder that this is not our home. We are merely passing through. While a 'passing through' can certainly seem like a permanent *settling down*, we are quickly reminded at the table of fellowship and feast that we are not settling down. It isn't over. We haven't seen our best days yet.

He throws His head back and laughs at the days to come, because our Groom is Christ. He knows the end of the story, and we win! We always win! Evil will cease and there will be no more pain, sorrow, suffering, or tears. One can become so weighed down with the heaviness of life, and so lost in the confusion of unanswered questions, that they quickly forget.

It is at His table and in our fellowship with Christ that He asks, "Are you having fun?" Only those who know the end of the story can laugh at the days to come. Only those who sit at His table can satisfy their hunger and quench their thirst. Only those who fellowship with Christ can find joy that outlasts all else.

13 CRUMBLING WALLS

It was a morning that I had waited, and prayed, to see. I had finally slept through the night, with better sleep than I'd had in a while. I woke up feeling completely rested, and ready to conquer the world. Then it happened! In a frenzy to get ready for work, and out the door on time, the shower wall literally crumbled underneath the weight of me!

I lost it. With an already-full day ahead of me, and a to-do list a mile long, I wondered how on earth I would get it all taken care of. On the way to work, fighting back tears, I said, "Lord I cry out to You in my frustration!"

I was finally at work, late, and not ready for this day that had already begun. I told a co-worker that it looked like 'Wreck It Ralph' came and showered at my place. I was trying to laugh it off, but instead, burst into tears because like that wall, for months I had tried to keep it together. That wall may have seemed strong on the outside, but the inside was a weak, soft mess.

Everyone reaches a point where enough is enough. The sudden death of my own brother; the unexpected death of a student I'd known for years, and then another friend back home, dead at thirty seven. Like the rest of them, he'd died altogether too soon. That was five deaths of people I loved in just one year. Throw into the mix my own chapters of darkness, that had taken their every twist and turn with such precision, it was almost predictable. I wondered, how much could a heart really take?

This had been a year of incredible loss. The last thing I found myself to be, on most days, was blessed to be in the name of the Lord. I'll be honest, I felt like that crumbling wall. If one more person had told me another Christian cliché to try and patch it up, I might have just crumbled even more.

Silence is only awkward when we don't say what we are supposed to say. There are questions for which we will never have answers. The greatest gift we can ever be to one another is to fully **be there**, whether it be the highest of highs or the lowest of lows; sometimes in silence and sometimes with a hushed prayer.

I had never known loss such as I'd experienced that year. After 30 years of knowing how to keep it all together, I'm slowly learning, rather, how to be undone. Because it is in the undoing of ourselves that rightly positions us for God to piece us back together how He chooses.

It is in the crumbling wall that we can find a Way Maker who never crumbles. It is my every last tear that He catches in a bottle. He *gets it*. Because He *gets it*, it just doesn't matter if nobody else does.

Life can be an incredible disappointment; but, it reminds us that we are merely passing through this place, onto something greater, somewhere greater with Someone greater, Who will never disappoint.

To those with crumbling walls, unending tears, nights with little sleep, and those trying to pick up the pieces of shattered dreams: you are not alone. There is a God who crumbles walls for His own glory, a God who has unending bottles to catch your every tear, a God who never tires or slumbers, a God who gives you dreams better than your own. There is going to be a glorious unfolding.

14 GIANTS VERSUS SKINS

I noticed it yesterday while on the upswing from a migraine that had me confined to my bed all morning. I saw a sign at the local wing joint that said, "Giants vs. Skins @ 8:30".

Then it hit me out of nowhere, like a jolt to my heart that awakened me to a greater reality. My mind flashed to young David: a mere shepherd boy, who had been anointed to be king, and yet reeked of sheep waste. His only job that fateful day was to take cheese and crackers to his big brothers, to just check on them. The anointed king had not yet been beckoned to battle. But we all know the end of the story, right? David could not stand to hear this mocking giant make fun of God's people, much less God Himself!

Stone. Sling. Slain giant. Yeah, it's "giants" versus "skins". Isn't that the theme of our lives as Christians? Sure, we are all just a bunch of *nobodies*, with our cheese and crackers, in the daily grind of our coming, going

30

and breathing. Yet, those with ears to hear are the ones who hear the soundtrack of heaven echoing in the background, with a great cloud of witnesses. The witnesses know, too, that it's *always* giants versus skins on this planet!

It's those *nobodies* who dare to be *somebody*, the somebodies who rewrite the history books of our time. It is because there are giants to be slain, and a kingdom to advance, and because love always wins! Today, we arise, and we go forth, because we always win, saints! We always win.

Don't ever stop taking your victory lap, even before your battle is won - because we always win. Giants versus skins ... can you hear the soundtrack playing?

15 A RED BENCH

A downtown street. A red bench in front of a rustic storefront. Resting my achy body, I am reminiscing. I am remembering a friend whose body will be laid to rest today - a young man who passed way too soon. While the questions echo louder than the answers ever will, one thing remains true: I am alive! In this moment, I am fully here, and fully alive; breathing, heart pumping, and brain synapses connecting at a faster rate than I can blink. It's rare I take moments like this to sit and be still.

Then she comes, sits down at the other end of the bench, and talks about her bad knees and tired body. I tell her I can relate. It's funny how the thing that holds us up can be the very thing that connects us together. She tells me she's from out of town, I tell her me too. My thoughts drift to Indiana, and thinking of friends and family who will gather.

Then He whispers, "Tara, tell her I haven't forgotten

about her." I casually dismiss this voice, thinking, "Surely, I've heard wrong." The echo of the voice grows with every beat of my heart, and its message I cannot deny.

A few moments pass, and she asks where a public restroom is. So, I take her into a store and show her the way. It's time to leave now. Will I live with regret, or will I die to self in this moment?

I ask for her name, and tell her that God wanted me to pray for her, to tell her that He has not forgotten her. She gives a courteous smile, as if to appease me, and says, "Ok, sure."

I pray, and say amen. Then the tears come, like the dam has finally broken, and she tells me. She says, "It's like you knew all along, how you just prayed for me. I just came from the funeral of my niece. She was 44, and died of cancer."

The tears run like a river, cleansing a heart of grief, and I'm reminded…reminded of a God who is so near He knows the most intimate details of our lives; reminded that when we carry a load not ours to carry, we'll feel it in our bones; reminded that His whisper can turn into a prayer, and a voice that speaks when all seems silent.

Reminded that my slowing down is somebody else's moving forward. It's ironic how the very thing that holds us up, is the very thing that connects us together. I am thankful for a God who sees it all, knows it all, and catches our every tear. We give a hug and say goodbye, and the God who whispers looks down with love so pure, and reminds us, He hasn't forgotten.

COMING HOME

16 A NEW SEASON

I arrived at the office unusually early this morning, the first brisk morning of the new season. While unlocking gates, getting ready for the day, I heard spaceship-like noises. A cluster of activity was happening behind the building. I noticed a crew laying new railroad tracks, and readjusting others.

That's when it hit me: laying new track is always part of a bigger plan, of something new to come! In a season that has left my heart with a layer of frost, and on most days a drink much too bitter to swallow, perhaps this is my greatest season yet. Perhaps the pain I have felt so deeply, the restlessness of my spirit, and the wandering of my mind, is nothing more than the laying of new track by a God who is up to working out His great plans for me (Jeremiah 29:11).

Everyone has heard it before, but it's the tough times that tend to hammer us down, shaping us into who we are. It's the fire that gets turned up that drowns out the dross and impurities of the gold. My greatest prayer in this season has been one of faithfulness; simply, "God help me to learn whatever it is You're trying to teach me!"

I can't tell you what it is exactly I'm supposed to be learning, but this morning I've received a clue: HOPE. The Word says that hope deferred makes the heart sick (Proverbs 13:12). I've had a sick heart for a long time. I have felt sick on the inside, while the outside did its best to keep it together.

This morning, as a new season blows in, and as I see grown men bundled up and shouting over heavy equipment while laying track as part of a new project and what's to come, I am reminded. I am reminded of a God who never grows weary or takes a break from His work; reminded that seasons come and seasons go; reminded that laying new track is part of a bigger plan; and reminded that I do indeed have hope, because my God never quits or walks away.

Maybe He's laying new track in your life too, or perhaps you've longed for a changing of seasons. Be assured that our loving, gracious God is at work, even on cold days while everyone else sleeps.

Hope, oh what hope! Here's to what's to come, friends - a new season with an unchanging God.

17 **TURNING TABLES**

Today I'm angry. I am angry about a lot. When there is a pot of water boiling on the stove, it only takes a potato or two to send it boiling above and beyond its capacity. That's where I am.

This morning my dog, sweet darling that he is, sent me over the edge, and he knew it. As if hiding under the bed he could escape from living in the same reality that I do.

I'm angry about injustice in the world, in our streets, and sometimes in our homes. I'm angry about feeling racist, when in all actuality I am not - but my skin is of a color that has been blasted the last two weeks. I'm angry about working my tail off, so others can sit at home and manipulate the system. I'm angry that grown adults bully others, because really, on the inside, they are nothing more than a hurting child who needs healing and freedom.

I'm angry at addictions that suck the very life out of

others, sometimes, in fact, killing them. I'm angry that millions of babies die every day, a majority of those dead because of a refusal to take ownership and responsibility. I'm angry that people lie, living in constant deception. I'm angry that sin hurts, and not just my own sin, but that of those around me. I'm angry that my entire life I've had a puzzle to solve and I hate solving puzzles, because there always seem to be a missing piece.

I'm angry that I have to be the bigger one; that if I really love Jesus, then it means climbing onto my own cross every hour of every day. It means dying to myself, because it's not just about me. The times that I don't die to myself, I am merely following a religion, a rigorous set of rules that I am bound to break.

I think anger is okay, but it's how we respond to it that makes the difference. Jesus was angry, walking into the temple, seeing the greed that had filled the air. The house of God had been turned into a marketplace. His response? Stunning. He overturns the tables, and begins to reestablish what it was always meant to be - a house of prayer.

So, today, I'm going to overturn a table. It will probably be later, with no crowd to witness. I am going to speak by faith, and with authority, just like Christ did, and reestablish some things. Because it takes a shifting in our hearts and minds, like that of an overturned table, that can take anger and give it the right momentum to help rebuild the kingdom of God - which is what we all desperately need.

Anger destroys and tears down, unless it's fueled in the heart of God, and then it rebuilds the kingdom of God here on earth. That's what I want to be a part of, even on my darkest days.

COMING HOME

18 **AGAINST ALL ODDS**

I've been chewing on Gideon the last few days. I just can't believe how ridiculous the details of the story are! God's ways are truly not our ways.

I am wondering what my response would be if I were in Gideon's shoes:

- drastic army cuts,
- downsizing of troops,
- sending thousands home right before the battle,
- fleece watching,
- fire consuming the sacrifice, etc.

But he never tripped, even with an army of three hundred against thousands.

Was it because he saw the hand of God at work? Because, when you see the hand of God at work, regardless of the situation, you know that He has your back. That's why **giving thanks in all things** is so crucial to your battle strategy! It shifts your perspective.

Pull a Gideon today. You are never outnumbered when you're with God. Just ask David.

19 **MOVING MOUNTAINS**

It was my first time at a ski resort. I loved the snow that was freshly gracing the mountains that surrounded us. There were people everywhere, zipping by on their skis, with face masks creating a winter masquerade.

I was dreaming of the day that I would strap on a pair of skis when I noticed him. It was a quick, fleeting moment that I would have missed, had God not allowed me to see him: a man in full ski gear, making his way in and out of the crowds of people. What set him apart from all the others was the fact that he had just one leg; one man with one leg on a single ski with two poles.

I don't know him, nor do I know his story. But it struck me - this man refused to be limited because of a setback. He refused to sit and watch while so many others did what he wanted to do. He refused to be another statistic of a bad chapter in the story of life that rarely makes sense; instead, he lived a different story.

What is beautiful about this thing we call life is that we don't have to live according to our setbacks, or be defeated by the things in life that come against us. Rather, we have this really huge God who calls us His own, and loves us beyond anything we could ever imagine! It is this same God Who says, "Listen, child! Nothing is impossible for Me."

I've been surrounded by mountains graced with snow, and while my lungs struggle to gather air into them, my heart also struggles for the kind of faith that moves these mountains. I, too, want to live above the odds; to live the story that God writes; to be the one whom others see and walk away inspired.

Thank you, sir, for your bravery to defy the odds, your courage to be different from the rest, and your reminder to live a story that only God can write - one of stunning impossibilities, breathtaking courage, and a journey of moving mountains ... even if it is only one leg at a time.

20 FAMILY DINNER

Saints, take care of your issues with brothers and sisters, no matter how petty, or even if they loom large. At the end of the day, we all sit down to the same table of fellowship with Christ. There's nothing more awkward than a family meal with dissension.

Break bread in peace, not bitterness.

COMING HOME

21 **REDISCOVERED HOPE**

Hope can be incredibly disappointing when it's not anchored in Christ.

Hope deferred makes the heart sick ... desperately sick. There is only One Who can make that sick heart whole and well again - Christ. When you allow Him to hold the broken, infected pieces of your sick heart, you rediscover *hope*, and your heart is on the mend.

Christmas bleeds with hope, because it is the unending story of a perfect, whole God who enters into the broken mess of humanity and says, "I AM here! I will be broken so that you can be made whole!"

He never disappoints.

22 SHARED SUFFERING

Christ doesn't invite us into His suffering for the mere purpose of suffering; rather, to remind us that there is fellowship in the suffering: Immanuel...God with us.

23 COURAGE

Courage! Oh, what courage can do! Like fresh wind in the sails, just a measly ounce of courage can multiply in God's Kingdom. Courage can cause walls to come crashing down with just the blast of trumpets, because courage knows that simple obedience is bigger than itself.

Courage! Oh, what courage can do! It can take a young lad and cause him to run head on into a giant that no trained soldier would fight. In the end, it wins, because courage knows that God always wins.

Courage can take a knife and raise it above a son's head on the altar, because courage knows that God always provides. Courage can build a boat when the land is dry, while people ridicule, because it knows that God always follows through on His Word.

Breathe deep, inhale courage, and exhale wonder … because a weary world is waiting to rejoice.

COMING HOME

24 A SACRIFICIAL GIFT

I've read it countless times. I have even told the story again and again to countless children. But it struck me just yesterday – Abraham was a man that God would bless, yet was trapped by his own impatience with God's promises. He and his wife took matters into their own hands. Somehow, even in the midst of our impatience, our grumblings and murmurings, our "fixing" of things, even our own wretchedness as sinners before a holy God, God keeps His Word. His purposes always come to pass.

Time passed. Abraham and his wife have their son, their promise from God fulfilled. Just when he thinks it's time to coast into the Promised Land of blessings, God gives him a test. As if being a parent at the ripe age of 100 isn't enough, God asks the old man, Abraham, to take his son up on the mountain to sacrifice him as a burnt offering.

The audacity of such a request! I can imagine the way

his heart must have sunk right out of his chest. Did he sweat? Panic? Punch a wall when his boy wasn't around? Was he even sure who he was trusting?

Abraham gave the wood to Isaac. He took the burning coals and knife, and the journey began. How does one step when he doesn't want to get to the end? But Abraham, old geezer that he was, walked by faith, and not by sight. The young boy caught on and asked his father where the lamb was, and Abraham quietly replied, "The Lord will provide, son."

They arrive, hearts racing, palms sweating. Abraham tied his son to the altar. What was it like for Isaac that day? Panic? Fear? Anxiety? Anger? Frustration? Feeling alone? Betrayed? We don't really know. While I've put myself in Abraham's shoes, or sandals rather, every time I've read this story, I've never thought about it from Isaac's perspective. As Abraham raised the knife, were there tears of anguish? Did he beg for his own life? Cry out for mercy? We don't know. All we know is there was faith and obedience.

The knife was raised - father to son. Then a messenger of the Lord spoke up and stopped Abraham. He turned and there in the thicket was a ram. This story would have been much different had Abraham known the ending; even, had Isaac known that it would be his back laying on the altar. It is striking that the ram wasn't provided until the very end.

But I'm challenged. Had I been asked to do that, either part, I would have bailed. That is radical faith, and most days my faith adds up to a hill of beans. Radical faith is what drives our hard obedience, and in turn brings about the mysteries and miracles of an Almighty God. That is the kind of life I want - one of incredible faith and pure obedience.

I don't have any children, but children are a gift from God. I've been thinking about the many, many gifts God has given me. Am I willing to lay those down? Can I take what is most precious to me and lay it on the altar before God? Do I trust Him to provide even when I cannot see what He is doing? When it seems as if I will lose my very life, do I know without a doubt that God is there ahead of me?

He is faithful when I am not. He provides when I'd rather not. When we are asked to lay down our very lives as a sacrifice, we can then turn and fully appreciate the Lamb that God provided, Jesus, who takes our place and becomes the sacrifice. In turn, our lives can become a gift back to Him.

TARA DAVIS

25 **MESSY COMMUNION**

There's a certain spot on Sunday mornings where I like to tuck away. It is somewhat of a hiding nook with the Lord. It is in the far back corner, last pew, a couple of feet in from the aisle. It is in the shadow of a fake tree... a really fake tree. It's typically pretty quiet back there, and I'm able to enjoy entering in to worship. In this place, in this little peaceful nook, I find myself refreshed when I leave.

Yesterday proved to be different, in some ways at least. We were singing a classic hymn, "Come thou fount of every blessing, tune my heart to sing Thy praise..." Suddenly, a family of 3 adults and 4 children came rushing in, cramming into the "holy space" in the pew in front of me. The serenity of my moments with the Lord seemed to fade away into the chaos of little children who were squirming for elbow room on the pew, along with parents who were desperate for their kids to straighten up, or for Jesus to come back in that moment.

Over the next twenty minutes, between finishing up worship and partaking of communion, every little thing that could have gone wrong...did! The girl's shoe fell off; the older boy was rambunctious and reluctant to make room for a sibling; the little girl slapped her momma and declared "NO!" again, and again. Just when all might be calm and bright, the middle lad dumped his communion down the front of his shirt.

I sat comfortable in my nook, thankful yet reflective. Communing with the Lord isn't always pretty.

I think sometimes we have this lofty idea that, "I'll sit and have peace for a few minutes, and a chorus of angels will sing above my head while I spend time with Jesus." We think it needs to look pretty, or be perfect. But I think 'the holy' is often right in the middle of our mess, and that communion is sometimes found right in the middle of our crammed communities.

Ask any mother out there, especially with young children, and they'll tell you what it's *really* like. Constant interruptions, and if you can sleep enough at night to get up at 5:30 in the morning, before the sun peeks over the horizon, and the phone starts buzzing, and children start asking for milk, you've beat the curve.

But in the midst of it all, we have grace. And all is grace because there is a God who so longs to be with us that He comes. He sits at the dining table as the child screams and He says, "Peace! I AM here." He runs dashing through the store with you as you buy only what you absolutely need, because the need is greater than the budget and He says, "I AM here! I will provide." He comes in the midst of spilled communion and dirty hearts, and says, "I AM here! I will cleanse."

Immanuel, God with us, in every moment of every day. He is Holy in the hushed, and holy in the hustle and bustle. All is grace if we will simply slow down and take notice. Communing with the Lord will at times be messy! There will be fear, unbelief, tears, anger, and a constant demand from the things around us that fill our lives.

However, communing with Him is always worth it! Because He always comes to give more, to be more, and to simply be God so that we can just be.

26 A ROYAL FEAST

It is a grand table, made of the finest of wood with gold embellishments. There are many, many chairs, but He pulls one out for me. A feast has been set out for the most royal of guests, the King. He treats me as royalty, as if I'm the only one in the room. Delicacy after delicacy, laughter, the peace is so thick in this place it's like breathing in oxygen. The longer I sit in His presence, the smaller my enemies begin to shrink. He prepares a table for me in the presence of my enemies, but it's His presence that casts out all others: fear, worry, anxiety, anger, pain.

We dine, we fellowship, we feast. I drink of His cup that pours out mercy. I eat of His bread, whose crumbs bring healing. Then we dance, we dance to the song of salvation. My King has rescued me. Not only has He saved me, He has redeemed me, restored me, and He calls me His own. I am no longer forlorn, no longer forsaken, no longer abandoned, but loved -- deeply loved, chosen, His favorite one.

Yes, You romance me, my Beloved.

27 A KINGDOM TO CARRY

I am His and He is mine. His very name is inscribed upon my dirty feet, feet that have quickly wandered into sin that has easily entangled. Even still, He calls me His own.

Jesus, the name above all names. Jesus, the name that carries power, freedom, healing, peace, joy, and love. His Name carries the very kingdom of heaven.

Sometimes the name embedded on the bottom of my feet can be covered over by the muck and mire, yet it remains. He remains. And wherever I step - my home, the office, the city marketplace, the crime-filled streets, the unbeaten paths - I carry His name. Because I carry His name, I carry the very kingdom of heaven.

How beautiful are the feet of those who bring good news! Every child of the King brings great news, one step at a time. Every road we walk, we usher in His power, peace, love, joy, faithfulness, and justice.

We carry the very kingdom simply because we belong to Him, King Jesus.

28 **BECAUSE JESUS**

Yesterday, I was with a group of students, teaching them about steps of faith, and trusting God. It was a simple object lesson to follow along with the Bible story that day. I asked a student if he trusted me. His response was, "I trust you Tara, because Jesus trusts you."

I was blown away by such a pure, innocent response. Who thinks of these things? I've been chewing on it ever since, trying to process it. The reality is *trust* is a hot button in our society. At the click of a button we can un-friend, block, unlike, and any number of things to another human being. Truth be told, these things hurt. They hurt, because more times than not, they come from the ones we'd least expect it from: friends, colleagues, childhood friends, sometimes even our own family rejects us.

What this little boy said yesterday spoke so much truth, and peace. What does it mean that Jesus, the very Son of God, the One who conquered death and the grave, *trusts me?* What if I don't want Him to trust me? How on earth did this fifth grader think such a thing?

These are three not-so-simple questions with three very simple answers:

- **Jesus trusts me because I am His**. I was made in His image which means I can be trusted. I can be faithful. I can do the right thing. If I am stretching out on a limb here that might not hold up under the weight of my own sin, the truth is that the times I fail or fall short, I chose it. I choose to not be faithful, to be selfish, or to do the wrong thing. Regardless, my own shortcomings never stop my Creator from full trust and confidence in me! That is incredibly humbling.

- **If I don't want Him to trust me, well that's just too bad,** because I am His: all of me for all of my life. I am no longer my own, for I was bought with a price. He is God, I am not.

- **This young boy is pure innocence**. The kingdom of heaven belongs to these little ones, because the reality is, the kingdom of heaven is a culture of honor. It is a safe place where we bring out the best in one another. He saw something that I didn't. Maybe instead of listing the reasons we don't trust each other, we could remember Who created each other.

Dig deeper. Find the thread of significance that runs in the robes of the royal and maybe, just maybe, because

God loves you then I ought to also. Because God trusts you, I can trust you.

The kingdom is never about us at all. It is all about our Savior and King, Jesus, Who picks up the towel and washes our dirty, grimy feet that have too often rushed quickly into sin. In so doing, He cleanses our hearts, and says we are forgiven.

When we pick up our towels and bend our knee to the ones around us in humility and service, we can bring out the best in one another. We can see the beautiful beyond the ugly, the whole beyond the broken, the trust beyond the betrayal. Because even still, in our wanderings and unfaithfulness to not only each other, but to Christ Himself, He still prepares a lavish table, and invites us to come and feast.

Thank you my fifth-grade friend, for speaking truth, and loving well. There is such peace, such joy, such healing in my heart…what a feast.

29 **RED LIGHT DISTRICT**

For far too long, My children have squandered themselves in the red light district. They have been chasing after broken cisterns that never satisfy, drinking the pleasure of their own wicked selves. They have been pursuing love in all the wrong places. These false gods of lust have promised to satisfy, but never kept their word.

Come to Me, My child. I AM love. I define love. I AM pure. I am right. I satisfy. I give. I love. I pursue. I chase down. I AM jealous with My love for you. I love you like no one else ever will. You are Mine! You will always be Mine. Whether you run into My longing arms, or stay wandering in the red lights of the darkest night, I beckon you.

I AM calling you. Listen closely. Can you hear My still, small voice above the chatter of the world? Can you see Me through the chaos of the streets? I AM here! I AM yours! You are Mine! Have your thirst quenched, your hunger filled. You long to be known, to be loved as you are.

I AM here! It is Me for which you long. Come drink deeply and be satisfied. I alone will fulfill your deepest longings.

30 **WELCOME HERE**

"Holy Spirit, You are welcome here..." The chorus echoed with grace in a room of what sounded like angelic choirs.

Then Holy Spirit began to speak to me. "Am I truly welcome here?" Because the Spirit brings life, yes. Comfort, of course. But what if He brings conviction? Is He welcome then, too?

The welcoming of Holy Spirit is actually an invitation for me to come and die. Die to self. Die to sin. Die to preconceived ideas. Die to little ideas of a much greater God.

Welcoming Holy Spirit is **not** an invitation to pick up a cross for it to be easily set down again when the weight of the burden is heavier than I had hoped. Rather, it is climbing onto a rugged, wooden cross that forever marks who you are, and changes the trajectory of your life.

My voice grows silent in response; yet my heart thrums

with the familiar chorus of what my flesh is too quick to ignore....HOLY SPIRIT YOU ARE WELCOME HERE. YES, HOLY SPIRIT. YOU ARE WELCOME HERE.

31 IT'S WHO I AM

The song played on, "Good, good Father," by Chris Tomlin. As I listened, I was so struck by the simple, Biblical sentiment behind it: our God is a good, good Father. That is Who He is. He loves us and that is who I am…I am loved. It is my Identity.

I've worn a lot of hats over the years, of which some I am proud: teacher, coach, children's pastor, daughter, sister, friend, mentor, evangelist, clown, athlete, and still others. Of course, there are the ones I am not so proud of: sinner, broken, bitter, angry, lonely, desperate, addicted, alcoholic, druggie, lover of self, pursuer of pleasure.

As I sit and write these thoughts, I can feel a switch in my heart: from simple joy reminiscing to shamefully dodging my past. The chorus plays again and I'm struck: At the very core of who I am, it's this….I am loved by God. A wave of relief washes over me and this truth echoes loudly in the shallow chambers of my heart, shutting the mouth of my accuser.

I am deeply thankful, thankful that in no way am I defined or devalued by any hat I wear; rather, I am marked by the love of the One who numbers my every hair. It is this truth that strips me down, day in and day out, rightfully setting my course.

Hats come and go and get lost in the breeze that blows, but it is God's Word that lasts forever! At my very core, at the very least, I am loved by God. It is enough...it's more than enough. Whether I agree, or understand, or always feel that way is irrelevant; it's true. As I am today, imperfections and all, I am loved by God, and that's who I am. It is more than enough, and I find myself deeply satisfied in Him.

32 WASTED WORSHIP IS WORTHY

Your anointed worship of Jesus can fill the house, giving others the sweet aroma of His presence. There are two responses: enjoy those moments with Him, or complain about the cost of such worship. One serves God, one serves man. God said you cannot serve two masters.

All too often I've found myself complaining about the cost rather than counting it all joy to honor the One who paid the highest price. Judas said these things not out of genuine concern for the poor, but rather, because he was a thief. When we try to take what doesn't belong to us, it gets everything twisted.

And yes, how often are we trying to solicit our own praise? Look at me, look at all I've done, look at what I haven't done, someone give me a pat on the back.

Don't take what's not yours. Rather, pour out again and again what is yours: your time, money, love, adoration, your very life. There is no cost too great to pour out our praise, our lavish love, on King Jesus.

He alone is worthy.

33 COME IN

I've been thinking about a house this morning. There's quite a difference between being "attached" to a house versus being "in" a house. Being attached symbolizes being outside, only peering in, perhaps wondering what could be on the inside. It doesn't take much commitment - as quickly as you are there touching the front door, so too, you can quickly leave.

But being in the house is a totally different story. You have full access, unhindered in every way. You can feed yourself, take comfort in a couch, see what's on the inside and what hangs on the walls, even get cleaned up. If you're in, you're in. There was an invitation - someone that initiated and said, "Come in." It means you are welcome here.

So it is with Christ. In John 15, He doesn't say abide on me. Think on me. Take time for me. No, rather He says abide IN me. It's an open invitation to explore, to have full access, to see what's on the inside of His heart, an invitation to come and feast.

When I approach my time with the Lord as a task or obligation, perhaps even out of fear or guilt, I merely stand at the front door, entirely missing the point. But when I recognize that it is He who opens the door and invites me in, it changes everything. Because it is *in Him* that I truly find my home.

The invitation to explore with Him is the greatest gift anyone could ever receive. All I have to do is walk through that door. Abide, because either you're in or you're not.

34 **WAKE UP**

Yesterday began with me going to bed at 1:30 a.m., only for an alarm to go off at 5:30 a.m., signaling the beginning of basketball tournament day. After coaching four games and wrapping up last minute details, I had driven another four hours to a hotel where I had crashed at 12:30 a.m. My alarm was set and would sound too soon at 4:30 a.m. to catch a flight.

Exhausted is an understatement. Friday's late night was simply because of pure fun. I have made it my mission to be more fully alive, and sometimes that means missing the standard ten o'clock bedtime. Last night's lateness was out of necessity. Anyone that knows me knows that I can sleep like a bear, hibernating for hours; however; there are times that require due diligence. I had just settled into a deep sleep when my alarm started its obnoxious call this morning. My first reaction was tapping that little glowing word that said 'snooze'. Then I came to my senses. The reality is, had I hit snooze, I would have missed it - my connection.

I think as a follower of Jesus this rings true too. I can't tell you how many times I've opted to "snooze" just one more time. How many connections have I missed? How many fully alive moments did I lose along the way? How complacent have I grown in my walk with the Lord? We are in an all-out war, and I am not referring to world events. There are literally lives that hang in the balance! How selfish of me to hit 'snooze' when, actually, God is calling me to action.

He is waking up His people, saying, "This is what matters." I am awake today in a way that I have not been. A familiar verse comes to mind that simply says this, "Teach us to number our days that we may gain a heart of wisdom," (Psalm 90:12).

That is my prayer today - no more snoozing through the battles. God has called me to action. He has enlisted me for this war and I now find myself more fully awake, fully alive, and covered in His grace.

Nobody ever hits snooze by accident.

35 PONDERING PRESENCE

Matthew 1:18-20

I am struck by something in this passage, something I've never seen before. Joseph could have stuck with his own plan - a quiet divorce, so as to avoid shaming Mary. The way it is written makes it even sound like his reputation was on the line, "He was a just man." His plan of action was based entirely on his own understanding of everything that was happening, which, much like our own, was small, and limited.

Can you imagine if he had followed through with his decision? After all, God created us each with free will. Eve followed her own plan, as did Cain, and so many others along the way. It was in his pondering that the angel spoke, and everything shifted. No doubt you and I each ponder things every day, in the secret places of our hearts. There are always voices that speak in our ponderings, but the question is: whose voice will we listen to?

God's ways are not our ways. His thoughts are not our thoughts. We can change the trajectory of human history, either for good or for bad through whose voice we listen to. We must be as diligent in our listening as we are in our ponderings.

36 STILLNESS IN THE WAITING

Waiting. I am still waiting. Waiting for that golden ticket, that perfect moment, the intertwining of our arms as we dance until everything else fades away in the distance. The chill envelopes my calloused heart as the world whizzes by. What I'm so desperately seeking I can't find: peace, love and joy.

The raging world maddens with every passing second, with beheadings and bodies washing up on shores, because there were too many left without a home. Rumors of war echo greatly in the human cavern of our weary souls. Where is the hope that we so desperately need?

Running from one thing to the next, because somehow it's the busyness of it all that distracts from the persistent ache we all feel. We simply keep posting, and pinning, and snapping, and tweeting, and believing this lie that we just don't have time. We are the gods of this universe that carry the unbearable weight of the world, and where is this supposed God anyway? Working on a cure for cancer, or saving marriages, or zapping the worst of us with lightning?

The rat race of 'self' continues, but it keeps adding up short at the end of every day. I break the silence with tears that cannot be explained. The mold is cracking, because somehow I was made for more.

Just when all seems dismal and gray and past the point of no return, I recognize that still small voice that I once knew. He says, "Come! I've prepared a table for you in the presence of your enemies."

I am struck. He has been here all along - my great Champion! The very One who breathes stars into the night sky, keeps the planets in perfect orbit, and hand-crafts each new sunrise and sunset. He has been waiting for me to draw near, to push past the darkness, and to keep focus in the dizzying chaos of life.

I've missed it again, but regardless of how many times I've missed it, He still remains. Once again, He extends an invitation to come and feast, to taste the goodness of the Lord, and to fellowship with the One who hasn't fallen off His throne.

Abide, it's more a posturing of the heart. And when your heart is postured, weary though it may be, everything else around you fades away.

37 PRISONERS IN GRAVEYARDS

The air had a chill in it - a chill that wakes even the weariest of bones. The clouds were a dismal gray, but it was the stripes of their uniforms that caught my eye. Prisoners! There were prisoners working in the cemetery. Their clothing spoke of their record, each having been convicted of some crime in the past.

Isn't it funny how we can run ourselves weary trying to forget our yesterdays, when all of our tomorrows will speak of how we've lived today. The fresh earth piled up next to a hole that awaited a corpse, and it was as if all of time stood still in that moment.

I suppose they are no different than the rest of us. All of us are just a prisoner to someone, or something, and working in this graveyard we call life. The reality is we all live, we all will die and we all have a record. Our lives are but a blur of a second in the vast reality of all eternity, while we aimlessly wander around chasing Pinterest perfect lives, one-upping the other on our social media sites. Really, in the end, none of that matters one iota.

Because one day fresh earth will be piled high, and your corpse will be laid low, and what really matters is how we live now. This is because someone, somewhere, is still not free. They still don't know Jesus; children still die without food to eat and babies are still senselessly murdered every day. We all just want our lives to count.

It's possible to move from prisoner to free. In so doing, we move from merely digging holes for dead corpses to helping others climb out of holes, bringing the dead back to life.

38 CRASHING SHORES

The grains nestled between appendages on weary feet. They say without toes it'd be impossible to stay on your feet. It was calm, serene, the storm clouds rolling off into the far distance. Inhale, exhale, and wait. I'd prayed my entire life for God to take all of the broken pieces and glue them back together again. Most days, it sure seemed as if He were unmotivated, too busy, or even maybe His glue dried up. But for once, maybe this was the calm in the storm that was needed.

The gentle waves ebbed and flowed, carving paths in the sand that altered the stubborn current. The sun hung perfectly over the horizon, casting its last rays of light into a darkening sky. Then it came, the wave that broke the peace and the current that swept away reality. It came crashing down with a force I'd never known. I struggled for air, gasping for a breath of hope in a world that completely flipped upside down! Sand castles everywhere were flooded with the force of nature and sometimes what you've worked so hard to build can be swept away in a moment's notice... and you're left clinging to the very grains upon which you once so firmly stood.

The broken pieces now shattered into a million fragments, impossible to fix. Every step is mixed with grains and shards: grains of grace that smooth away the calloused places, along with shards that cut into new areas. The blood mixes with salt water and there's a cleansing that comes with the burning. All is not lost, after all.

For it is in the continual ebb and flow that strips the shore of its formality, and sometimes the same current that beats one helplessly to the very ground from which it came is the same current that reveals treasures yet to be seen. Looking for treasure in the midst of tragedy, I am thankful the salt reminds me I am alive. I am not overcome.

39 THE JOURNEY HOME

Sometimes one can forget where one is going. It's as if the countless "U-turns", the annoying yields, and the constant red lights of life can stop you dead in your tracks. All of a sudden you've forgotten where exactly you were headed.

It is then, in the retracing of your roots, that you are reminded of who you are, and who you're **not**. It's in the studying of the family tree that you recall who it is that God has created you to be. Just one glance at the map and everything is reoriented; this is who I am, this is who you are, and this is where we are going.

Sometimes it's a drive down memory lane, a familiar sight that jogs the dazed memory of a yesterday far removed from our current reality. But it is those *yesterdays*, every last bit of them, that have shaped your *todays*. And your *todays* will carve the path for your *tomorrows*. Soon, you'll wake up and realize that even in the midst of a wrong turn and a failure to yield, there's been a God who has been laying new stretches of road on which to journey. He knows that He created you for adventure - adventure with Him. Anything less than that is second best, and second best will forever lose, because nobody wants second, ever.

So onward, friend! Though the path may be lonely and dark at times, the reward in the end will be well worth it. While others chase after idols that will eventually break, you are chasing the One who will always satisfy. While others lose sleep chasing dreams full of nothing, you are living dreams full of everything and losing sleep!

Only those who run to win the prize will win in the end. Everyone else will shed tears of remorse over their ribbons that say, "Nice Try"! You will receive the crown of life and hear from the One Himself, "Well done, good and faithful servant."

This is the journey home, the adventure for which you were made.

40 **WHEN TWO BECOME ONE**

It was the softest of whispers, the quickest of glances.

Your smile lit up the room like the most magnificent of sunrises on the horizon.

One look into your eyes changed everything. It was in those eyes that I saw love: raw, unhindered, relentless love.

A love that I had never known, had never tasted.

You stretched out your hand and took hold of mine, beckoning me to dance while the music never ends.

We spun and we twirled, tossing back our heads in decadent laughter that danced with the rhythm of our hearts; it was just you and I here in this sacred place.

As if that weren't enough, you had still more in mind.

The most lavish of feasts prepared, an extravagant spread of the finest in the land, an invitation to come and dine and nourish ourselves on each other's company.

In the land of the living and the land of the dying and in the midst of monsters raging all around, you invite and I respond.

This is the 'Yes' I've been waiting to declare my entire life! This one 'Yes' cancels all the other 'No's that have been stamped on my heart.

Because it is your unfailing love that emblazons the seal upon my heart! The seal of your covenant love that will never fade, never die, never diminish, never run out, and never grow weary, because your love is relentless! You never stop chasing me down to love me - just as I am.

You keep chasing, and finally I've stopped running away! I leap into your arms full of grace, because there is no other place I'd rather be than here with you, and you with me.

There's a beautiful merging between the two of us. What was once two has now become one, and we are better together.

Completing me, you fill in the empty spaces and caverns of my heart that I never knew existed! You make me who I am.

Yes, you make me who I am.

We dance until there's no more left of today. We have the rest of tomorrow which will span into all of eternity.

The dance will never end, the song will never fade, the engraving of my heart by your hand will never wash away because I am my beloved's, and He is mine.

I am seen, I am known, I am loved.

Cherished, treasured, held close, enveloped in the presence for Whom I was created.

COMING HOME

41 **WARRIOR**

The wind is whipping harder now. The skies are growing darker with every passing minute. The enemy continually fires off rounds in what feels like the not-so-distant surroundings. Some, once so full of life, now lay lifeless, an empty shell. Some have hidden in holes, paralyzed by fear of the unknown. Others have quit, exhausted beyond repair. Just because you wear the outfit and carry the gear doesn't make you a soldier.

Everyone plays pretend now and again, even adults, but I have set my face like flint towards my enemy. I am unmoved. I will not retreat, back down, or consider anything that's less than true. The battle rages on, but my Commander does too, and He is the One who goes before me. He champions the way for all of us to follow, we need only trust Him. Trust Him when it seems impossible; follow Him when the way is unknown; hold out for Him and how He will work, even when it seems as if He's not concerned. I'm not in it for the accolades. Those pretty things don't exist on battle lines. I'm in it because the odds are in my favor, and I have nothing to lose. If God be for me, then who can be against me?

This is who I am, a warrior. His blood runs through my veins. His destiny is written in my DNA and I will not back down. Always moving, always advancing, never quitting. I've learned I must fight His way in order to secure the victory. So I pray. I pray for the one who wronged me. I forgive. I trust. I wait expectantly, waiting with hope. I move forward, though the attacks seem stronger and louder. I call my enemy on his bluff because I know the end of the story. And I win. We always win.

Rise up warrior! Finish your fight with heart.

42 CAGED

I love the zoo. It is one of the few places where I can feel like a kid again. There's something about watching God's creations in their habitat that's magical. It reminds us of the miracle of life itself that we so often forget with the chaos of today.

Yet, I find myself a bit sad when visiting zoos. While the animals are well taken care of, and their environments are as closely matched to the real thing as possible, it's still not what's best. Caged animals, free in a sense - and yet not.

Sounds a lot like humans. Created to be free, to run and to live this grand adventure of life, yet we all are caged in some way. Held back by our own fears, limitations, or the sin to which we keep returning. Jesus paid a ridiculously high price, far beyond anything we could ever fully understand. He did that so we could be free: free from the hate, the pride, the racism, the division and the sin that never satisfies. Yet we stay in our cages.

I wonder what life would be like if we dared to venture beyond the confines of our cages, and joined the adventure with our Creator.

ABOUT THE AUTHOR

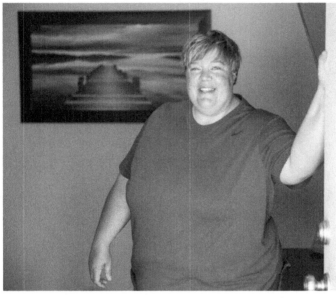

Reading, writing, and speaking gives Tara life. Having spent nearly a decade wandering from the heart of God and into a life of bondage, it was the love of Jesus which would ultimately set her free. Her story of redemption, freedom, and new life is woven into every facet of her writing.

Tara is a gifted storyteller, using everyday examples, raw life lessons, and humor to reach hearts. Her audiences include all ages and range from overnight camps, graduations, to church events. Her passion is Jesus, her gift is storytelling, and her purpose is simple: to make much of Jesus.

Pursue Christ always, everything else is rubbish!

Made in the USA
Columbia, SC
20 January 2018